FROM THE BEST-SELLING
Power of a Positive™ SERIES

S0-AAJ-222

The Power OF A Positive Woman

HOWARD PUBLISHING CO.

GIFT EDITION

Karol Ladd

Our purpose at Howard Publishing is to:
- *Increase faith* in the hearts of growing Christians
- *Inspire holiness* in the lives of believers
- *Instill hope* in the hearts of struggling people everywhere

Because He's coming again!

The Power of a Positive Woman, Gift Edition © 2004 by Karol Ladd
All rights reserved. Printed in the United States of America

Published by Howard Publishing Co., Inc.
3117 North 7th Street, West Monroe, Louisiana 71291-2227
www.howardpublishing.com

04 05 06 07 08 09 10 11 12 13   10 9 8 7 6 5 4 3 2 1

Cover and interior design by LinDee Loveland and Stephanie D. Walker

ISBN: 1-58229-356-2

Let's embrace our
uniqueness
as women,
recognizing that we were created
with distinctly feminine
characteristics.

   1

From Eve to Mary to Mother Teresa,
God has had a unique plan
for women on this earth.
He created us with His own definition
in mind, using our

womanly strengths

as well as some of our female flaws
to paint an eternal picture.

Let's hold dear the fact that we are
wonderfully made by God.
And let's relish the

heritage

we have as specially fashioned
creatures designed for a unique plan
and purpose in this world.

 3

You are God's specially formed
workmanship, designed by a

perfect Creator
and loving Father.
You wear a designer label embossed
with God's own fingerprint.

4

What is unique about you?
Name some of the

qualities and gifts

God has given to you.
In what ways can God use your
strengths for a greater purpose?
Make a list and dream big!

Wonderful Creator,
thank You for the unique qualities
You have given women in general
and for the specific characteristics
You have given to me.

Thank You

for the way You have used women
throughout the ages.

Please use me now
to make a positive and eternal
impact in this world.

Life isn't perfect.
Circumstances aren't perfect.
And people aren't perfect.
But the good news is that

God is a perfect fit

for our overstretched,
out-of-balance, more-than-slightly
imperfect lives.

If we want to be
positive women,
we must look daily
to our heavenly Father for strength,
support, and direction. He is more
than able to work in us and
through us despite our
imperfections.

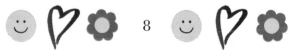 8

We need to maintain a
healthy balance
in our lives by releasing those things
we were never meant to control in
the first place! We need to pry our
hands off the things only
God can control and look to
His strength and power
to take care of them.

9

Immediate gratification
can rob us of

joys

to be received
or lessons to be learned
from God's deeper,
more thorough plan.

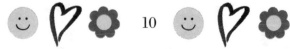 10

Take comfort in the fact that
nothing is too hard for God!
Trust Him
with your greatest longings,
your deepest needs,
and your strongest doubts.
He is with you,
and He sees far beyond what you see.

Spend time alone with God
for the specific purpose of releasing
your life to Him.

Ask Him

to reveal areas where you tend to
demand control. Release these
areas to Him, asking
for His power and strength
to walk forward with Him at the
control panel of your life.

Dear Lord,

mold me with Your powerful touch.
Fill me with Your wonderful Spirit.

Allow Your work to be done in my
life, using both my strengths and
weaknesses for an eternal purpose.
I trust You to faithfully lead me
because You are my loving,
heavenly Father.

13

We may not always know God's
purpose for us. He doesn't reveal
His intentions all at once. But

step by step,

as we walk with Him,
we will find that
He faithfully leads us
according to His plan.

We may have times
when we are
unable to understand
God's thoughts or discern His plan,
but we can still
trust Him.

When the storms of life
rock our boat,
our faith in God allows us to

rest our full weight

in His safe and loving arms.

Great
women of faith
have journeyed down this road
before us, keeping their eyes
steadfastly on Jesus.
They were able to stay the course
because they cast off the things that
entangled them and
ran with diligence
to the finish line.

When did you first take a step in
faith toward God?

Write

down your story
so you can share it
with your family and others.

Wonderful heavenly Father,
help me
to walk in faith,
trusting You for the big picture of life.
I may not understand all that You do
or allow, but I trust Your loving grace
to see me through every
circumstance. Lead me step by step
in faith as I follow You.

When we put our
faith in Christ,
our lives go through a
spiritual makeover.
As we become women of faith,
our behavior begins to change
to reflect our newfound beliefs.

Could there be a lovelier, more positive woman of faith than one who is clothed with compassion, kindness, humility, gentleness, and patience? Who bears with others and forgives them? Who exudes love and peace? A woman wearing such an outfit would be asked continually where she did her

shopping,

and the answer would be
"At the feet of Jesus."

We may never be famous
or have an opportunity to influence
thousands of people, but if we each

walk in faith

right where God has placed us,
together we can
make a positive
difference in this world.

22

Faith

is stepping forward as God directs,
even when we don't know what the
outcome will be.
It's doing something bigger than
ourselves—so big that we are

dependent on God

and not on our own strength
and ability.

23

Most of the positive women of faith in
the world today are women we have
never heard of. They are sweet,
humble women who walk a life of
faith step by step,
day by day.
They may never achieve fame, but
they are making
a positive difference
in the lives of the people around them.

Is God telling you to
step out in faith
in a certain direction? Are you
holding back because of fear,
anxiety, or lack of self-confidence?
Remember, where we are weak,

He is strong.

Step out in faith, and watch Him
work through you.

Giver of life,

thank You for changing me and
making me a new creation in You.
I want to honor and glorify
You in all I do and say.
May my faith be evident as a result
of Your work in me.

Wisdom

is a type of application of the
knowledge we possess.
It is not knowledge
in and of itself.

A wise person

makes decisions based on the
understanding that God and His
time-honored principles are the
only sure foundation
in life.

Wisdom is a great deal more than intellectual awareness. It involves knowledge, yes, but also discretion, sound judgment, and all the rest. Most importantly, wisdom includes a healthy **fear of the Lord.**

29

When we find wisdom,
we become
positive women
capable of having
a powerful
impact on our world.

Do you love wisdom?
Embrace it.
Passionately pursue it from the
God of wisdom Himself. You will

obtain blessings

that are lasting and eternal in value.
A woman of wisdom
is truly adorned with life's
greatest jewels.

Pursue wisdom by sitting at the feet of the giver of wisdom, God Himself.

Decide on a time

each day when you will read and meditate on His Word. Commit yourself to pulling up a chair at the banquet table of wisdom and tasting its delicious morsels daily.

God of all wisdom,
how wonderful it is to go to You for
wisdom, direction, and comfort!

Help me to grow

in wisdom so I may be a woman of
wisdom and a woman of Your Word.

As positive women,
we want to be

purposeful

about the direction
we are going
and the means we use to get there.

Success

doesn't lie in having all of the
answers about our future; it lies in
following God's direction
day by day.

 35

The Bible

is our flashlight as we journey down
the path of life. It leads us and
guides us in truth
and steers us from false and evil
ways. It provides nourishment and
strength along the trail.

36

If you come to a fork in the road,
after wise consideration and prayer,

start walking

down the path that seems the wisest;
then make the best of it and
leave the results to God.

Most roads have
challenges,
twists, turns, joys, and sorrows.
Just because we hit a bump or meet
a roadblock doesn't mean we made a
wrong decision—otherwise every
person in the Bible went
down the wrong road!

Write out

a strategic plan for
the rest of the year.
Remember to seek God's direction.
As you set your goals, reflect on
those areas of your life that may
need a direction tune-up. Ask God
to help you in these areas.

Father, help me to
trust You
and not simply lean on my
own understanding.
Help me to acknowledge You in all my
ways as You direct my paths. I want
to be a woman of wisdom, direction,
and discretion, living a life that
honors You in both word and deed.

40

God is just and loving,
and He is waiting for us with open
arms and a listening ear.
He stands before us saying,

"Come to Me,

give Me your burdens, and
find rest for your souls."

Our real
reward
comes in investing in the
things that won't fade away.
Investing in people,
drawing near to God,
living according to His Word,
and sharing it with others:
These are activities worth seeking.

What are you seeking?
To what do you

devote

your heart, mind, soul,
and strength?

Reflect on what you strive for in your
life. You may find you need to
readjust your direction. Seek wisely,
because you most likely will find
what you seek!

A "yes" answer to our prayers

doesn't depend on our holiness or goodness.

If it did, we might become prideful when God answers us or judgmental of others when their petitions aren't granted. Remember, even Christ got a no to His request to "let this cup pass from Me" (Matthew 26:39).

We can be
confident
that prayer changes things,
because God changes things.
Never underestimate the power and
lasting influence of a
positive woman's prayers!

Begin each day with
prayer.

Then in every situation that day, before fretting or becoming discouraged, pray and ask for God's help and direction. Make this a moment-by-moment practice, walking hand in hand with God throughout the day.

I praise You,

loving and kind heavenly Father,
for hearing my prayers.
In faith I reach out to You,
offering my love, my obedience, and
my requests. Thank You for
answering my prayers in the way
You know is best for me.

 47

Isn't it wonderful to realize that
the God of the universe
is close at hand?
We don't have to travel to distant
lands or the deepest regions
of space to find our great
and mighty Creator.

As positive women, let's
determine today to
spend more time
thanking God and reflecting
on His work in our lives.
If we do, we'll begin to see a
difference in our attitude toward life.

It is easy to think
prayer
is a small thing to do for
someone, when in fact it is
the most powerful
and positive thing we can do for
another human being.

Pray for God to work in
ways you can't even

imagine.

Always do what you can to help
others, but make sure your prayers
are included in your help.

 51

Oh the joy of
releasing
all our worries to God!
A positive woman is one
who knows this secret of a
happy Christian life.

Decide today on
a time and a place
where you will meet with the Lord
in prayer. Begin the time by reading
Scripture and praising God,
thanking Him for His care.
Then share your needs with Him.
Take time to listen to Him too.

Loving Father, I often try to carry
too many burdens and worries on my own.

Help me

to give these cares over to
You on a daily basis.
Help me to be faithful to meet with You
and enjoy the sweet fellowship of Your
love, Your Word,
and Your presence.

Happiness is nice, but it's temporary.
Joy is something different altogether.

Joy
is a constant.

It's not dependent on circumstances
or people but rather on a heart issue.
Happiness is external;
joy is internal. Joy can be tucked
deep in the heart, even in difficult
circumstances.

There are times in our lives when we may have joy without a smile. Then,

evidence

of our joy may be found in our words.

Words of kindness, gratitude, and praise represent a joyful heart, while words of gossip, grumbling, and complaining reflect quite the opposite.

A positive woman is a
joyful woman, and a

joyful woman

has a powerful effect on
the people around her.

Joy is more than a feeling;
it is a deep

peace,

blended together with a solid hope
that God has not left us.
Joy is a delight in knowing
there will be a better day.

In this life we are going to have
happy times and sad times.
But at all times, we can
be positive,
joyful women, because we have our
heavenly Father's assurance:
It's better higher up.

Write out

a "happy list" of things you enjoy.
Now write out a "joy list" of reasons
you have to rejoice in the Lord.

Compare the two lists.

Often things that make you happy
are based on temporary enjoyment,
while your reasons for joy are based
on things that are eternal.

Glorious heavenly Father,
You are the giver of joy.
Thank You
for the joy Your Spirit produces
in me. Forgive me for covering
up or hiding my joy at times
when I should allow it to shine forth.
Help me to share
this joy with others.

No can be one of the most positive
words in your vocabulary
when it comes to your
schedule.
Know your limits.

You will gain much more
respect
from doing a few things well
than from doing a myriad of
activities halfheartedly.

Talk

to your heavenly
Activity Director.
If God is the one doing the
stretching, you'll grow stronger
in the process. If He's not,
you're sure to pop
like a rubber band.

64

We must distinguish between the **thoughtfulness involved in serving others,** which is healthy, and giving in to people's thoughtless demands, which can be unhealthy.

As positive women, we need to focus
on developing these four areas of life
in balance: wisdom, stature, favor
with God, and favor with mankind.
All four are important. Think of
them as the four legs of a chair;
if one is missing,
balance
is difficult to maintain.

Draw a picture
of the sun and clouds.
On the sun, write "The joy of the
Lord." Describe what this means to
you. On the clouds, list areas in your
life that tend to hide the joy that's
inside you. Ask God to help you
diminish these clouds so
His joy can shine through.

Wise and wonderful God,
forgive me

for the times I've been too busy to
enjoy the sweet fellowship that comes
from spending time with You.
Help me to balance my time and my
life wisely and carefully, and show me
how to set things right so my joy will
overflow once again.

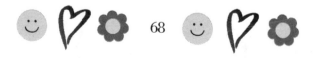

Top Seven
Relationship
Ingredients

1. Take a genuine interest in others.
2. Be a giver, not a taker.
3. Be loyal.
4. Be a positive person.
5. Appreciate the differences in others.
6. Build on common interests.
7. Be open, honest, and real.

69

Every person has an invisible sign
around his or her neck that reads,
"I want to feel
important."
Everyone has something to offer
this world. We need to search for it,
find it, and bring it to the surface.

What can we give to others?

How about a smile,

a hug,

a kind word, a listening ear, help with an errand, a prayer, an encouraging note, a meal? We can come up with many things to give others if we are willing to be attentive to their needs.

    71

Positive women demonstrate an
attitude and a spirit that
sees God at work in all
of life and

encourages

others to see Him too.
They are generous with praise,
with smiles, and with love.

Make three lists:

(1) acquaintances, (2) good friends,
and (3) best friends.

Pray for your friends, and ask God to
direct you to a person who may
eventually move to the next list.

Take steps to deepen your friendships—

for example, make a call, write a
note, or set a lunch date.

Father, not only have You told us in
Your Word how to love, but
You've shown us how to love
through Your Son's example.

Thank You!

Help me now to share
that kind of love with others and
to be a reflection of Your love
in all my relationships.

What people really need
is to see
love in action.
Love in action boosts people to
greater heights of development
and growth than words
or good intentions alone.

Every act of
love,
great or small, noticed or unnoticed,
makes a positive impact
in the world.

Love has many faces.
It displays itself

uniquely

in and through each individual life.

At times the most
compassionate
thing we can do is to
confront a friend
or loved one and then offer a step
up—a lift to help the person move
forward in a positive direction.
Kindness should be coupled
with wisdom as we speak
the truth in love.

Ask God to direct you to one area of
service or ministry through which you
can show His love to others.
Ask Him to open up an

opportunity

that will best utilize your
unique gifts and talents.
Then actively pursue that opportunity
to show His compassion to
the people around you.

   79

Compassionate heavenly Father, may my life be a **reflection** of Your love! Help me to love others as You have loved me. I thank You that Your love is complete in kindness, compassion, service, and truth. Help me to show Your love and compassion to the world.

 80

Faith

in an all-powerful God
goes hand in hand
with courage.

When we choose to move
courageously ahead, we are actually
putting our faith into action.

Courage

takes us out of our
comfort zones
and into magnificent places we
could never reach on our own.

Some of us are called to be active
and speak out like Susan B.
Anthony, while others are called to
quietly hold strong like Rosa Parks.
Whenever and however we
take a stand,
we must do it prayerfully
and with wisdom.
And we must do it with
love and kindness.

We may not know we have the courage
to face a challenge until that challenge
comes. In ourselves we are weak;
we are clothed in human frailties.
But God promises us that
when we are weak,

He is strong.

Courage is His work in us.

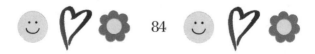

Write a letter

of encouragement to
one or two people
who need courage right now and let
them know you are praying for them.
Next, think of an area in your own
life in which you need courage.
Ask God to strengthen your heart.

Lord, thank You for promising that You
will never leave me. Although I may not
always understand Your ways,
I can always depend on Your

faithfulness.

Help me boldly step out in faith,
following Your direction.
May my life, my actions, and
my courage bring glory to You.

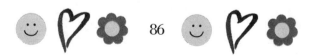

Fear tends to grip all of us in different areas and at different times in our lives. When we allow it to get the upper hand, it captures us in its net and keeps us from experiencing the

abundant

and fulfilling life God intends for us.

You and I have
no guarantee
that the next moment will be free
from tragedy. We only know that God
will not leave us, whatever comes
our way, and that
He is working all things
together for good.

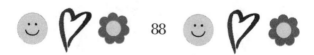

If you will trust yourself to God's
wise guidance
and loving care,
He will help you make
it down that mountain of fear and
into the valley of peace, joy, and
abundant life.

89

God is with you,
positive woman of faith!

Fear not!

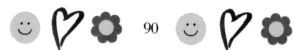

Identify

areas in your life that are stifled by fear. What actions or precautions can you take to help reduce your concerns?

In prayer, deliver to God those factors that are out of your control.

Relinquish them to His hands, trusting Him for the outcome.

King of heaven, thank You for
reminding me in Your Word to not
be afraid, because You are with me.

Help me

to face the fears in my life
that keep me from moving forward in
faith. I relinquish them to You
and ask You to replace them
with Your peace.

Hope

is not simply a sense of expectation,
because you can expect good things
or bad things to happen. No,
hope is a yearning for
something wonderful
to happen;
it is looking forward to the best.

The hope of the cross is
powerful.
It is the hope that Christ paid
the price for our salvation.
It is the hope that Christ rose from
the dead and that the same power
that raised Him from the dead
is at work in our lives.

Grumbling is an unproductive use of
our time, words, and energy.
When we whine and complain,
we encourage doubt instead of faith.
We take our eyes off of the

hope

we have in God
and place them on immediate issues
and temporary things.

95

When we lose hope,
we sink.
But even then God is there
to lift us up; we just have to reach
out for His hand.

Write
a statement of hope.

Make it a personal reminder, based
on God's truth. Place your statement
of hope in your Bible and refer to
it whenever you need to be
reminded to get your eyes off
of your immediate circumstances
and back onto Jesus.

God of hope, I praise You.

Renew

my hope and help me to
keep an eternal perspective.
Today and every day, help me to
choose an attitude of hope rather than
an attitude of gloom or despair. Teach
me to be joyful in hope, patient in
affliction, and faithful in prayer.

How do we encourage someone along life's pathway? How do we hand out hope? The answer begins with simple steps—small acts of encouragement and kindness based on our

recognition

of the other person's great value and worth in God's eyes.

When we share the gospel,
our words become a

message of peace

to those who are restless,
of love to those who are angry, and of
hope to those who are hopeless. We
offer them healing and wholeness as
we share the good news that they,
too, can be reconciled to God.

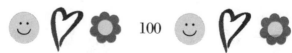 100

We don't have to be celebrities or national heroes to have a positive impact on others.
We only need to offer
encouragement
through our caring smiles, our loving touches, our words of hope, and our supportive cheers.

When we get our eyes
off ourselves and
**pour our lives out on others
in words and actions
and cheers that**
inspire hope,

we can't help but become more
hopeful too. And that's when we
become truly positive women.

102

A content woman is one who accepts
the people and the circumstances
around her and makes the best of
her situation. She has an

inner peace,

leaving to God those
things she cannot change
and making a difference
where she can.

Celebrate
what's right in your life.
Enjoy what you do have. And most
importantly, enjoy being with the
people who are dear to you.

The power of a
positive woman
is not your power;
it's God's.

Feed delicious morsels of hope and

encouragement

to your family and friends every day.
List specific ways you can do this
for each person. Then ask God to
show you someone outside your
circle of friends to whom you can
be an encouragement.
Pray for that person daily.

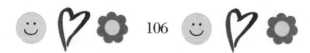

I love You, Lord!
Help me to continue moving forward
in my walk with You.

Tenderly teach

me and guide me along the way and
help me to make positive choices
each day. Help me to press on for
Your glory until the day
I meet You face to face.

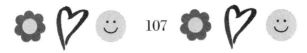

We only have to live
our lives one step at a time.

Perseverance

is the key
to reaching the finish line.